Original title:
Cosmic Coffeehouse

Copyright © 2025 Creative Arts Management OÜ
All rights reserved.

Author: Maxwell Donovan
ISBN HARDBACK: 978-1-80567-876-2
ISBN PAPERBACK: 978-1-80567-997-4

Celestial Captivations

In a realm where stars do sip,
Mugs are filled with nebula drip.
Galactic laughter fills the air,
Who knew that stardust brewed with flair?

Planets spin on coffee rings,
While aliens dance and munch on wings.
Lunar lattes, frothy and bold,
Serve tales of the universe untold.

Saturn's bands swirl like cream,
Martian mischief, a caffeinated dream.
A barista with antennae serves high,
While comets zoom past, oh me, oh my!

Jupiter's moons play hide and seek,
While rocket poets rise to speak.
With each sip, the cosmos ignites,
In this funny world of starry delights.

Cosmic Conversations

In the corner, a star starts to chat,
With a moon who's wearing a tall, silly hat.
They sip on some nectar, brewed from the sun,
While debating if planets can dance just for fun.

A comet swings by with a wink and a grin,
Telling jokes about black holes and how they spin.
The galaxies giggle, twinkling bright,
As laughter spreads out into the night.

The Coffee of Infinity

A cup so grand, it holds the whole sky,
Sipping wisdom as constellations sigh.
With each little sip, the universe gleams,
Pouring out dreams like impossibly sweet creams.

The beans from a planet where humor's the trade,
Make jokes about gravity; all jokes are made!
The milky way stirs in its frothy delight,
While planets wink softly, in dark velvet night.

Planets in a Teacup

Inside a teacup, a world spins around,
With Jupiter dancing and Saturn just bound.
They swirl in their brew, what a curious sight,
While Earth does its waltz, and the asteroids bite.

Mars laughs and it says, 'Take a sip of my dust!'
And Venus chimes in, 'Oh come on, you must!'
With steamy adventures in each little sip,
They toast to the space, giving chaos a trip.

The Dreamy Brew

In a cafe within a cloud made of dreams,
They serve shiny mugs that sparkle and gleam.
With a dash of stardust and giggles galore,
Every sip takes you to places unknown, evermore.

Black hole espresso makes time disappear,
While nebula lattes promote cosmic cheer.
With each frothy swirl, the universe beams,
As laughter erupts and dances in streams.

The Coffee Constellation

In a cup floats the Milky Way,
Beans that dance like stars at play.
Cream swirls like a comet's tail,
Sips of laughter, brew won't fail.

Caffeine rockets off the charts,
Each sip tickles budding smarts.
A galaxy of flavors burst,
Who knew that coffee could quench the thirst?

Starstuff Steeped

Steeped in dark, rich mystery,
A cosmic blend, no history.
Galactic grinds in swirling pools,
Awake the dreams of caffeinated fools.

Jupiter's beans, so bold and strong,
With every sip, you can't go wrong.
Uranus' brew, with a subtle flair,
Mug-shaking giggles fill the air.

Chasing Comets with Coffee

Chasing comets with my mug,
Sipping light-years in a hug.
Each gulp sends me spinning fast,
Just a sip—who needs the past?

Pours like meteors across the sky,
Laughs erupt, oh my, oh my!
Fleeting flavors race the night,
In this brew, we find delight.

Eclipse Elixirs

When the moon dips in the brew,
Twilight flavors, something new.
Dark roast whispers silly dreams,
While light bursts in frothy streams.

Sip the shadows, dance with glee,
Starry smiles for you and me.
Eclipsed by laughter, joy divine,
With every cup, we intertwine.

Comet's Kiss

A comet comes to sip and swirl,
With frothy clouds, it starts to twirl.
It catches starlight in a mug,
And laughs as planets give a shrug.

With sugar from the moons above,
This drink is crafted with great love.
Each swirl within the silver stream,
Is mixed with laughter and a dream.

Milky Way Morsels

Slips of stardust on a plate,
Twirled with whimsy, oh, how great!
A sprinkle here from Saturn's rings,
Delightful bites the cosmos brings.

We munch on meteorite treats,
While chatting 'bout celestial beats.
A dash of humor in each crunch,
A galactic giggle for our lunch!

Beans Among the Stars

Beans that twinkle, beans that shine,
They brew with dreams, oh so divine.
A cosmic blend of light and sound,
In every sip, joy can be found.

With jests exchanged, the orbs unite,
As laughter echoes in the night.
We raise our cups, a toast so bold,
To all the stories yet untold!

Ether and Espresso

Espresso shots from space's brew,
A zingy twist, a galactic view.
Sipping thick with stars above,
The universe made fresh with love.

Jokes fly like meteors in flight,
As we enjoy this cosmic night.
Each sip ignites a merry cheer,
In caffeine's warmth, we shed our fear.

Drifting Through the Dark with Decaf

In the void with no caffeine,
Stars twinkle, yet I stay keen.
Galaxies spin with sleepy grace,
Drifting slow in this vast space.

Sipping brews that float like mist,
A mug of dreams I can't resist.
Planets dance in espresso flow,
Decaf vibes are all I know.

Brews of the Andromeda

In Andromeda, they brew a lot,
Coffee beans from a moonlit pot.
Baristas mix with quirks and charms,
Galactic froth that warms like arms.

Asteroids roll with flavors bold,
Java stories often told.
Sipping stardust through a straw,
Raising cups in cosmic awe.

The Universe is Brewed

The universe brews in a kettle wide,
With flavors swirling, hard to decide.
Supernovas burst, then leave a stain,
Like coffee spills on a starry drain.

Nebulae swirl in creamy froth,
I can't resist, I take an oath.
To sip the stars, to drink the night,
With every cup, I take a flight.

Milky Brews

In the Milky Way, the beans do dance,
With each sip, I'm in a trance.
Coffee comets zoom past quick,
Laughing loudly, time to pick.

I hear a joke from a caffeinated star,
Telling tales of who we are.
With every laugh, we brew a bond,
In this funny space, we can respond.

The Milky Way Café

In a café with a starry view,
Baristas brew the cosmic brew.
With moons that dance on plates of cheese,
And shooting stars that giggle with ease.

Asteroids sip their mocha delights,
While comets argue about their flights.
In this place, time takes a break,
And black holes serve a wicked cake.

Cosmic Conversations

Aliens chat over lattes so warm,
Debating if gravity causes a storm.
With donuts shaped like planets so round,
In this space station, joy is found.

Galaxies gossip, swirling with flair,
A nebula joins, with pink curly hair.
They laugh at Earthlings, so stuck in the grind,
While sipping on slushies they find intertwined.

Espresso of the Stars

A barista winks, pours thick espresso,
While meteors lounge, discussing the best show.
The steam rises up, it tickles your nose,
While glittery cups spill tales that nobody knows.

Planets twirl with cups full of bling,
Sipping on new, out-of-this-world spring.
Each sip's a journey, a cosmic delight,
With every joke, they soar into night.

Interstellar Infusions

Sip on a brew that's light-years ahead,
With flavors that dance, and laughter widespread.
Sipping stardust in a swirling whirl,
With each caffeinated laughter, planets twirl.

Nebulas swirl in a berry punch,
As quasars join for a snack-time crunch.
In this café where the universe spins,
Every grin is a moment that wins.

Quantum Quench

In a cup of swirling dreams,
Particles dance, or so it seems.
A caffeinated black hole's might,
Sucking in my will to write.

Stirring spoons like comets fly,
Sugar cubes lift off the sly.
Baristas in lab coats mix,
Espresso shots, their cosmic tricks.

Lightyear Lattes

Milky Way creamer swirls in sight,
Travel fast, takes off in flight.
Next stop? A galaxy of foam,
Where whipped cream planets call me home.

Sip the space-time, love the buzz,
Warp speed on caffeine, just because.
In this nebula of mugs, we glide,
Stars align as laughter's tide.

Shooting Star Sippers

Catch a star in your espresso,
With every slurp, it feels like fresco.
Sipping dreams from cosmic mugs,
Each gulp a hug from space, it tugs.

Planets orbit our lively chat,
Laughter bounces, just like that.
Galactic beans, a roasted find,
Sipping stardust, oh, so kind.

Cafe of the Cosmos

In the café of the great unknown,
Galactic vibes, we've overgrown.
Java brewed with a comet's tail,
Laughs explode like a supernova gale.

Each table's a starship, ready to sail,
Hilarious tales perpetually prevail.
With every sip from the cosmic blend,
The universe is ours to mend.

The Espresso Nebula

In a galaxy quite bizarre,
Beans were flying in a jar.
Roasting stars with a sizzle,
Creating brews that'll make you giggle.

Planets churn with cream and foam,
Galactic lattes feel like home.
Asteroids dance with a frothy flair,
Making smiles float in cosmic air.

Celestial Concoctions

Orbiting around a cup so wide,
Sipping stardust with a side.
Meteorites in milk doth swim,
A carnival of caffeine whim.

Black holes stir with a frothy twist,
Every sip, you can't resist.
Jupiter's punch, oh what a taste,
In this universe, we won't waste.

Cosmic Caffeine

Aliens served with a side of cream,
Rockets launch with a caffeine dream.
Brewed in comets, hot and bright,
Every gulp's a delight-filled flight.

Lunar lattes, blissful sips,
Gravity's pulled by our joyous quips.
Zany zips in a swirling mug,
Joy explodes with every snug.

Alternate Universes in a Cup

In a dimension made of beans,
Cats serve coffee in moonbeam scenes.
Sipping laughter, chai and glee,
Every cup's a jubilee.

The espressos twirl and twist with flair,
While martian jazz fills the air.
Coffee grounds with time to spare,
Across the cosmos, joy we share.

Brewed in the Stars

In a café on the moon, quite bright,
With astronauts sipping with delight.
They laugh with glee, stirring their brew,
While zero gravity flips their view.

Saturn's rings serve as the cups,
Jovian giants dance, as time erupts.
A barista made of stardust and charm,
Brews the elixir with cosmic calm.

Planets paint the walls with coffee art,
Each sip takes you deep, deep in the heart.
Nibbling on comets, sweet and round,
As laughter and stardust swirl all around.

So grab your mugs, take a trip,
Through galaxies where flavors flip.
With a smile and a wink, join the fun,
In this café where all are one.

Celestial Creamers

Nebula swirls, full of delight,
Dimensional donuts take flight.
A sprinkle of starlight on frothy tea,
Makes every sip feel like glee.

Galactic flavors, bold and bright,
With Martian marshmallows, pure delight.
The comets race for the cream,
Sipping across the interstellar beam.

Baristas twirl like supernovae,
Serving lattes in a new way.
Gravity's just a suggestion here,
While laughter and sips echo near.

Every cup holds a secret star,
Sip slowly; don't spill, it's a far-off spar!
With each joke brewed, the universe grins,
In laughter's embrace, the fun begins.

Aurora Amaretto

Swirling lights in a cup so fine,
A drink that dances, so divine.
Iced constellations with a twist,
In this drink, you can't resist.

Bubbles pop with a joyful cheer,
As quirky creatures gather near.
A sip sends you to distant skies,
With every gulp, laughter flies.

Frothy clouds on a whimsical ride,
Creamy dreams on the cosmic tide.
Chocolate asteroids, crunchy and sweet,
Satisfy cravings with every beat.

In the realm of the amusing, we toast,
To airships of whimsy, we love the most.
With cups raised high, let's share a laugh,
In this brew of joy, we find our path.

Astro Beverages

Rocket fuel served in a fizzy glass,
Hitch a ride on this caffeinated pass.
With asteroids bouncing, laughter ensues,
As we sip on the fun that we choose.

Lunar lattes float like dreams,
While cosmic cupcakes burst at the seams.
Galactic giggles fill the air,
In a space where joy is everywhere.

Planetary punch with a twist of lime,
Time's a joke; we laugh at the climb.
So navigate your way to the bar,
Where the drinks taste better when bizarre.

Martian mugs hold tales untold,
Each sip a feeling, a memory bold.
In this place of intergalactic cheer,
Raise your mug, the fun is near!

A Sip Through the Stratosphere

Up above the clouds we sip,
While gravity takes a funny trip.
A latte made with stardust foam,
In this cafe far from home.

Planets twirl just like our cups,
As we giggle at gravity hiccups.
A barista dressed like a rocket ship,
Serves espresso with a cosmic whip.

Jupiter's ring donuts on the side,
As aliens dance in a merry glide.
Coffee beans from Mars on toast,
We laugh and cheer, toasting the most.

With every sip, the stars align,
Each cup tells tales of the divine.
In laughter brewed with every cheer,
We sip the cosmos, far and near.

Brewed in the Beyond

A brew from a star, bold and bright,
Sipping starlight in the evening light.
Baristas wrapped in spacey garb,
Making caffeine from a comet's barb.

Galactic mugs, swirling tales,
While meteors deliver cosmic sales.
Pancakes shaped like little moons,
As we sway to interstellar tunes.

Sipping black holes, swirling down,
Watch the hopeful faces frown.
Did I just taste a supernova?
Or is this just a hot cup of drova?

Laughter echoes through the void,
Every sip, our minds deployed.
With laughter and a cup in hand,
We toast to dreams across the land.

Coffee and Comets

Comets streak through our coffee scene,
Floating flavors, bright and keen.
We sip on darkness, swirl in light,
With every gulp, our futures bright.

A brew that's brewed from ancient rocks,
As we revel in celestial shocks.
Coffee beans with a cosmic twist,
In this place, nothing's amiss.

With caffeine, we plot our flight,
To Jupiter, and maybe Mars tonight.
Galaxies swirl in our mugs so grand,
We spin tales with every hand.

Sips as fast as comets race,
In this universe, we find our place.
In laughter, we discover the truth,
That coffee's magic lies in our youth.

Celestial Conversations

In a galaxy where coffee brews,
We sip on tales, share the news.
The sofa's soft, the laughter loud,
Our cosmic chatter draws a crowd.

Stars are our lamps, shining bright,
Beneath the moon's soft, silvery light.
With every cuppa, stories flow,
Of interstellar highs and lows.

Coffee spills lead to laughter spills,
Our cosmic dreams give us the chills.
Sipping brews that sparkle and pop,
As we plot and plan, we'll never stop.

Nebulas swirl, our minds take flight,
In this odd café, we own the night.
From milky ways to distant springs,
In laughter, we find the joy that sings.

Universal Infusions

In a café on Jupiter's ring,
Robots serve lattes with a zing.
Martians sip cocoa with a grin,
While Venusian baristas dance and spin.

Comets pass by, leave trails of foam,
Spacebeans brewed far away from home.
Aliens chat in a spangled haze,
Sipping stardust in a milky daze.

A black hole brews a dark roast blend,
Gravity pulls, but laughter won't end.
Cosmic customers all agree,
This place is the best in the galaxy!

In cups of light, they find their cheer,
With cosmic jests only they can hear.
They toast the stars with a joyful clink,
In this interstellar coffee drink.

Brews Beyond Borders

In a shop where comets crash and collide,
Espresso machines with nowhere to hide.
Saturn's rings serve up almond milk,
While nebulae pour cream as smooth as silk.

Pluto pops in, says, "I'll take a shot!"
He orders a brew that hits the spot.
A wormhole waiter stumbles with glee,
As intergalactic patrons sip with esprit.

Earthlings share tales of mocha misdeeds,
With alien tales of strange cosmic breeds.
A galaxy's worth of flavors to play,
Sipping a rainbow at the break of day.

Each cup tells a story, each sip has a twist,
In this zany café, nothing's amiss.
So take a seat, let the universe swirl,
And join in the laughter that makes the stars twirl.

Starship Steeps

In a starship café flying through space,
Teacups wobble with a lively grace.
Aliens argue about chai and brew,
While robots blend green tea like a pro do.

A cosmic spill makes a nebula mess,
Zipping through orbits, oh what a stress!
But laughter erupts, they take it in stride,
In this wild coffee haven, they take pride.

Asteroids crash, but spirits won't wane,
They serve up giggles like a sweet sugar cane.
Martian milkshakes bubble and pop,
Caffeine-infused fun just won't stop!

With every sip, the mysteries grow,
Traveling through galaxies, putting on a show.
So snag a cup full of joy and surprise,
In this starship café, laughter never dies.

The Universe in a Cup

In a chalice of stars, they stir with delight,
Brews from the heavens shining so bright.
Andromeda serves a latte so fine,
While Orion crafts teas of a celestial line.

Planets gather 'round for an evening toast,
Jupiter's brew is what they love most.
But Mercury's espresso is hot as the sun,
One sip and the giggles have only begun.

A milky way swirl in every sweet sip,
Black holes are filled with cosmic quip.
The cosmos in cups, they chuckle with glee,
The universe brews, just wait and see!

So here's to the laughter that binds us tonight,
In this endless expanse of pure delight.
With every celestial drink, a smile unfurls,
In cups full of magic, we sip and twirl.

Astral Aromas

In a space where lattes glow,
Buzzing beans, they steal the show.
Saturn's rings stir in my cup,
While Jupiter laughs, 'Hey, fill it up!'

A nebula swirls around my brew,
With hints of stardust for a view.
Martian muffins, flaky and light,
They launch my hunger into flight.

Venusian vanilla, oh so sweet,
With a sprinkle of quasar for a treat.
Black holes bubble in the blend,
A laugh from Pluto, just around the bend.

So raise your mugs, let's share a joke,
As comets dart like caffeinated smoke.
In this realm of sips and cheer,
Galactic giggles, bringing us near.

Galactic Grounds

In the café where meteors meet,
I sip on mocha, oh what a feat!
Asteroids dance like sugar sprinkles,
As I make jokes, laughter crinkles.

Astro-bagels toast to a crunch,
While aliens join me for a munch.
A latte art of a UFO,
Served with wit, it steals the show.

The space-time blend becomes my muse,
Beneath the stars, we can't refuse.
With cosmic creamer, planets swirl,
Big Bang chuckles, watch them twirl!

So grab your cups, let's orbit wide,
The universe giggles, deep inside.
With every sip, a little fun,
Under the sun, we're all as one.

Interstellar Infusions

Cup of stardust, steaming bright,
Takes me on a silly flight.
A comet drifts, my napkin flaps,
Galactic jokes, we share the laughs.

Time warps with each herbal blend,
As quarks and caffeine start to bend.
A black hole swirls, it pulls me near,
'More espresso!' sounds like a cheer.

Celestial donuts make us grin,
Around the universe, we spin.
With Milky Way cream, so divine,
Life could be worse, with this starry dine.

So join me here, let's crack a pun,
Beneath the stars, we've just begun.
With every sip, we'll laugh and play,
In this brew-tiful cosmic café!

Solar Flare Sips

Solar sips that make me glow,
Like a supernova on the go.
I giggle with my solar flare,
As caffeine fills the galactic air.

Extraterrestrial teas are quirky,
Some sip with spoons that are quite jerky.
Asteroid slices, tasty and bold,
Each bite a story, waiting to be told.

The coffee nebula brews delight,
Stars wink as I take a bite.
Giggling suns dance in my cup,
As I trill, 'Hey, refill it up!'

So let's toast under shooting stars,
With mugs raised high, no need for cars.
This jovial journey makes us beam,
In our funny universe, life's a dream.

Sips of the Supernova

In a nebula, I take a gulp,
The beans are brewed in a cosmic pulp.
Gravity's got nothing on my brew,
With each slurp, I float into the blue.

Jupiter's coffee is a little too sweet,
One sip makes me dance on my feet.
Saturn's rings just twinkle with cream,
A galaxy of flavors, it seems like a dream.

Black holes can't swallow my joyful shout,
With every refill, there's no doubt.
I sip on stars, oh what a delight,
This space café shines through the night!

Galactic giggles spill all around,
In this café, laughter knows no bound.
So grab your mug from the interstellar rack,
Let's sip through the cosmos, then head back!

Asteroid Aromas

On a rock adrift in the starry night,
Coffee aromas give such delight.
A comet's tail wags with each brew,
As meteorites crash—who knew?

Starbucks is nice, but this is a treat,
Asteroids serve up the finest heat.
I'll take a mocha drenched in stardust,
That cosmic kick is a must!

Sip it slow, let the flavors swirl,
Around this space bar, watch the galaxies twirl.
Earthlings may grumble, but we just cheer,
For asteroids brew like they don't have fear.

Cosmic cane sugar, I sprinkle it well,
Jumping from Mars to Jupiter—what a swell!
With giggles and sips, we fly around,
In the asteroid belt, joy abounds!

Sidereal Sips

Beneath the stars, we sip with glee,
No one can see that we spill our tea.
Milky Way mug, filled to the brim,
Watch out, dear planets, we're starting to swim!

Supernova latte? What a joke!
I ordered a regular, not this smoky cloak.
But here we swirl in a heavenly haze,
Caffeine in galaxies, oh what a phase!

Quasars bubble, giving us cheer,
Aliens laugh, "Have another, dear!"
Lunar lattes, oh what a flair,
We giggle with joy in the cosmic air.

In this starry café, fun reigns supreme,
From solar filters to a sparkling beam.
So raise your cups, let the cosmos flip,
For weird coffee fun on this stellar trip!

The Distant Decaf

Far away in a star's warm glow,
I crave that cuppa, but oh no!
Decaf they say, with a wink and a nod,
"It's light as a feather," I scoff and applaud.

Astronauts chuckle at my bold request,
In zero gravity, I strive for the best.
But sipping decaf in the void's a plight,
Space still can't quench my coffee delight!

The distant cosmos just gave me a quirk,
Dark roast I want—nothing will work!
With starlight twinkling, I roll my eyes,
At this caffeine-free joke in disguise.

But hey, the space dust does taste quite grand,
With sweet meteorite sprinkles at hand.
So join me now, in this decaf spree,
In a universe where giggles run free!

The Milky Way Mocha

In a galaxy far, far away,
Beans dance to the barista's sway.
Planets swirl in a frothy whirl,
As stardust lattes make taste buds twirl.

Black holes brew in endless delight,
With a sprinkle of meteoric bite.
Sugar comets zooming on by,
Sipping bliss while planets sigh.

Saturn rings made of cinnamon twist,
Cosmic sips you can't resist.
Aliens laugh as Earthlings sip,
In a mocha ride, take a trip!

Coffee clouds drifting so high,
With every gulp, the stars comply.
Galactic laughter fills the air,
In this caffeinated cosmic affair.

Deep Space Drips

Journey through the blackest night,
With drips of joy, a pure delight.
Starships zoom with mugs in hand,
Coffee on the go, it's truly grand.

Asteroids hopping in the brew,
Whipping cream like nebulae do.
Space-time bends with every pour,
Galactic flavors you can't ignore.

Gravitation pulls at every sip,
Like wormholes in a coffee trip.
Just a splash of martian flair,
Makes deep space drips beyond compare.

So raise your cup to the vast unknown,
In interstellar cafes, we're never alone.
With each drop, we sip and soar,
Traveling the universe forevermore!

Nebula Nectars

In swirls of color bright and bold,
Sweet nectars from the heavens unfold.
Bubbles rise like distant stars,
Each sip, a journey to Mars.

Cupfuls of joy, mixed just right,
Twinkling flavors, a dazzling sight.
Comets whiz past with a giggle,
While we sip and sing, caffeine's wiggle.

Galactic grooves in every taste,
No time for waste, let's not be chaste!
With alien snacks and cosmic cheer,
Nebula nectars bring us near.

So grab a cup, let laughter fly,
As stars wink down from the velvet sky.
Every sip a spark of fun,
In this universe, we're all one.

Quantum Coffee Quest

On a quest through quarks and beans,
Seeking flavors in dreams and scenes.
Each sip a theory, a space-time leap,
In the quantum world, coffee runs deep.

Baristas mix with particle flair,
Creating brews beyond compare.
Anti-matter froth swirls in delight,
A caffeinated dance through the night.

Time travel sips, a jittery spin,
With every gulp, we create a win.
Sip, swirl, and watch the waves,
In quantum cafés where laughter braves.

From photons vibing in the cup's glow,
We laugh and sip, let the good times flow.
In the tapestry of cosmos, feel the zest,
For every coffee quest is simply the best!

Astral Brews and Beans

In a realm where stars ignite,
Beans brew tales into the night,
Whispers of caffeine delight,
Sipping dreams till morning light.

Galactic mugs with foamy tops,
Rocket fuel that never stops,
Barista comets do the flips,
Laughing while the black hole sips.

Java jets and moonlit pies,
Wormhole lattes, cosmic highs,
Planets swirl in frothy skies,
With every sip, the universe flies.

So join the fun, take a swirl,
In the space where giggles twirl,
Every drink a new adventure,
Starry nights with laughter's censure.

Hyperspace Happenings

Brewing chaos in a cup,
Space-time bends, can't give up,
Orbiting with sips so bold,
Stirring joy, a treasure gold.

Mocha meteors shoot by,
Espresso skies, oh me, oh my!
Jumping through the flavorful bend,
Funny faces, laughter blend.

The aliens serve a quirky brew,
With jelly donuts, sweet and blue,
Gravitational coffee grounds,
Tickling taste buds all around.

As the stars begin to wink,
We raise our cups, enjoy, and think,
What a ride through hyperspace,
With every sip, we love this place.

Celestial Caffeine

Celestial bubbles rise and pop,
Mug in hand, we just can't stop,
Coffee planets dancing bright,
Underneath the moonlight's sight.

Sipping on stardust lattes,
Wishing for interstellar play,
Comets crashing, cups on high,
Laughter bursts as time flies by.

Space-doughnuts circle round,
Filling voids with sugary sound,
Jokes brewed up, steaming hot,
In our galaxy, we plot.

With each giggle, we explore,
Fantastic realms, we adore,
Take a sip, make it last,
Caffeine dreams, a cosmic blast.

Universes in a Mug

In a mug, a universe spins,
With frothy tops and silly grins,
Beneath the stars, we take our place,
Sipping joy in this vast space.

Time flies by in espresso shots,
Black hole donuts tie the knots,
Saucer saucers, giggling light,
Creating worlds, oh what a sight!

Each cocoa swirl a galaxy,
Twirling through infinity,
Bantering with the beans we brew,
Laughing as cosmos bids adieu.

So gather round, let's have some fun,
In our mugs, the joy's just begun,
Universes collide and bloom,
In every sip, dispelling gloom.

Moonlight Mochas

Under a sky of twinkling beans,
Stirring laughter with caffeine dreams.
Jupiter's donuts, oh so sweet,
Aliens tap-dancing on their feet.

Baristas serve with a wink and grin,
While Martians giggle, sip, and spin.
A latte art that looks like me,
Or maybe Elvis, can't you see?

Sipping stardust, feeling fine,
A sprinkle of comets in my brine.
Saturn's rings hold croissants galore,
Who knew space could have such a score?

From coffee thrusters, laughter soars,
Warp-speed banter as the memory pours.
In this café of the universe wide,
Let's brew our joy, with stars as our guide.

Wormhole Whispers

In a café tucked between the stars,
Galactic gossips, sharing bizarre.
A wormhole opens for a cake,
Time warps flavors, make no mistake!

Espresso shots from time's embrace,
We drink the past at a frantic pace.
Cheesy jokes from light-years away,
Aliens laugh, forget yesterday.

Asteroid pastries float on by,
"Try the green one!" the robots cry.
A quick sip turns to cosmic cheer,
As meteorites bring laughter near.

With each particle that we consume,
The universe hums a playful tune.
In this dreamy haunt, we twist and twirl,
Join the fun, let our minds unfurl.

Cosmic Cup of Comfort

In a nebula of sugar and spice,
Every sip comes with a splash of nice.
Stardust sprinkles on my scone,
Banking jokes that make you groan.

Galileo's brew, bold and bright,
Mars' mayhem seems just right.
Cosmic giggles dance in the air,
With foam mustaches, the joy we share.

Astro-rovers baking bread,
Yummy flavors fill our head.
With a wink and a splash, we spill,
Spacecapades to quench the thrill.

Sipping comfort in zero gravity,
Where smiles fly with every cavity.
In this delightful cosmic fest,
We serve laughter; it's coffee's best!

Celestial Foam

In this interstellar café's glow,
We serve a latte that steals the show.
Galaxy swirls in a frothy cup,
A sip will make your spirits erupt!

Milky Way marshmallows drift around,
While giggling comets twirl to the sound.
A celestial barista, juggling beans,
Toasting space-baked peanut butter scenes.

A whipped cream comet splatters wide,
As shooting stars slide and glide.
"Tickle my taste buds!" an alien cried,
With each slurp, the universe pried.

From cosmic brews to playful bakes,
Every giggle is a joy that wakes.
In this foam-filled laughter dome,
Let's sip and dream, we're far from home.

The Great Galactic Grind

In a café 'neath the stars so bright,
Aliens sip their lattes with delight.
A barista with tentacles makes a fuss,
Serves up drinks in a flying bus.

Jupiter orders a giant mocha,
While Saturn shakes its rings for a soda.
Mars claims it's getting frothy up here,
With an espresso that quenches cosmic fear.

A comet whizzes by with a grin,
Stealing sips, it zooms in a spin.
Venus just laughs, tossing cream in the air,
Space is a party; there's laughter to share.

In this café, the universe swirls,
Each drink concocted with giggles and twirls.
Galactic jokes brew up with each sip,
Join in the fun, take a cosmic trip.

Ether and Euphoria

In the ether, where dreams collide,
A bubbly barista, full of pride.
Mixes joy with a dash of tea,
Space-time bends with every cup, you'll see!

Mars and Venus shuffle on the floor,
Sipping smoothies, craving more.
A black hole slurps down a cosmic shake,
While shooting stars join in for goodness' sake!

Syrups swirl in flavors profound,
Galaxies spin as laughter resounds.
A sprinkle of stardust, a twist of fate,
Whirls through each cup, oh, isn't it great?

Caffeine comets zoom past your seat,
Awakening dreams, oh so sweet!
Join in the fun, let your spirit fly,
In this cafe, the universe is sly!

When Planets Percolate

Planets dance on the café floor,
Brewing laughter, who could ask for more?
Saturn spins as it stirs its brew,
While Mars juggle cups, it earns a woo-hoo!

Jupiter jokes with a frothy grin,
While Mercury dashes, craving a win.
A galactic blend with a splash of fun,
A hilarious race, who'll be done?

The Milky Way slips in with a cheer,
Ready for a taste, loud and clear.
Each drink a riot, flavors untold,
Where sips ignite laughter, bold and gold.

With every cup, the cosmos sings,
Galactic giggles, oh what joy it brings!
So gather 'round, take a comfy seat,
Prepare for fun in this cosmic suite!

Black Holes and Brews

In the corner, a black hole brews,
Sucking in photons, sharing its blues.
With coffee so strong, it's quite absurd,
One sip and galaxies spin, unheard.

The universe spins as laughter flows,
With comets crash-landing, nobody knows.
Asteroids dance on the floor with glee,
As cappuccinos float, wild and free.

Neptune's in line for a wild espresso,
While Pluto dreams of a sweet pistachio.
Planets chat over cups half-full,
Creating a ruckus, that's the pull!

The laughter swells, it fills the void,
In this café world, we're all overjoyed.
So grab a brew and join the fun,
In the cosmos' heart, no need to run!

Portals of Percolation

In a café among the stars,
Baristas mix the milky bars.
Jupiter's espresso is quite bold,
While Saturn's latte warms the cold.

Aliens dance with mugs in hand,
Sipping brews from every land.
A comet plops into the pot,
And suddenly the coffee's hot!

Nebulas swirl in frothy foam,
Every cup feels like a home.
With jokes from Mars and jokes from Mars,
Laughter echoes near and far.

So raise your mugs to the sky high,
Sip stardust lattes, don't be shy!
In this place where gravity bends,
The fun of brews never ends!

Dark Matter Drips

In shadows where the coffee flows,
Dark matter brews, nobody knows.
With secret ingredients from the void,
Each sip leaves every heart overjoyed.

The barista winks with a sly grin,
Spoon in hand, ready to spin.
"Do you prefer light roast or dark?"
An astrophysics question, let's embark!

Gravity's pull and caffeine's might,
Keep us buzzing through the night.
As quasars dance in the cup,
We sip our dreams, who needs to sup?

From wormholes built with foam so grand,
To little stars that fill your hand.
In every drip dwells a joke,
In every roast, the universe awoke!

Brews from Beyond

Galactic beans from distant skies,
Frothy blends with colorful vibes.
Moons mix milk into a swirl,
While comets chase a coffee girl.

Sip a brew from a supernova,
Taste the magic of a soda cola.
Time leaps in a caffeinated spin,
As black holes pull us further in.

With rocket fuel in every cup,
We levitate, floating up.
Cosmic mugs chatter, jokes ignite,
In this strange café, we take flight.

So gather 'round, you caffeine fans,
Where espresso dreams abound in pans.
Lets toast to brews that know no bounds,
In this place where joy resounds!

Stellar Sip Sessions

Underneath the starry dome,
We sip our drinks, we feel at home.
Uranus serves a spicy brew,
While Venus offers caramel too.

Black holes capture the best of jokes,
As Jupiter brews for all the folks.
Drinks are shaken, laughter flows,
Even meteors stop to pose!

Warped time means no hurried rush,
Here in space, it's all a hush.
With cosmic cream and alien puns,
Every sip is born from fun!

Our cups toast to the great unknown,
In this laughter, we have grown.
So swing by our galaxy café,
Where every drink makes your day!

The Dark Roast of Infinity

In the void where beans collide,
Black holes sip their java wide.
Galaxies swirl with a caffeinated twist,
Brewed up in the cosmos, too hard to resist.

Supernovae drip with espresso flows,
Planets juggle cream as the comet glows.
Time bends slightly as the roast gets bold,
A universe buzzing, tales yet untold.

Aliens brew amidst bright constellations,
Debating the perfect caffeine creations.
Laughter echoes in the starlit night,
While quasars shimmy, oh what a sight!

From gravitational pull to the final sip,
Each slurp a leap of a cosmic trip.
With every cup, a new story unfurls,
In this dark roast realm, laughter twirls.

Whispers Among the Stars

Under moons where shadows play,
Stardust whispers, 'Let's brew today!'
Jupiter's beans, a hefty grind,
Send galaxies giggling, oh so refined!

Martians sip on their frothy haze,
While Saturn's rings toast in bright displays.
A comet dances with a sugar rush,
While suns waltz by in a caffeinated hush.

Constellations chat over mugs of light,
Stars giggle softly, sparkling bright.
With a spoonful of joy and a dash of play,
They brew up dreams of the Milky Way.

Interstellar jokes in every cup,
With a wink and a grin, they all erupt.
Laughter collides like a cosmic tease,
In the warmth of blissful, starry ease.

Stardust and Sugar

A sprinkle of sugar on a nebula wide,
In cups of magic, the cosmos abide.
Twinkling snippets of laughter arise,
As meteors crash, creating sweet pies.

Milky Way mochas and lunar lattes,
Buzzing with fables of Martian cafes.
Stardust sprinkles on each frothy crest,
Galactic giggles put caffeine to the test.

With every sip, galaxies jive,
Supernova smiles keep the joy alive.
Bubble up laughter with every stir,
And watch the universe happily purr.

Planets play tag with steaming mugs,
Sipping laughter like giant hugs.
In this bizarre brew of cosmic delight,
Sugar and stardust make everything right.

Galactic Grounds

Amongst the stars where the beans take flight,
Galactic grounds serve laughter bright.
Asteroids dip in the caramel sea,
While black holes joke, 'Come sip with me!'

Nebulae froth with whimsical dreams,
Turbocharged brews fuel cosmic schemes.
Suns chuckle as they roast for fun,
While comets zip by, each on the run.

With every pour, adventure starts,
In this buzzing realm where laughter imparts.
Quasars beam down a joyful ray,
To each cup of joy in this milky display.

Dimensions twist in caffeinated cheer,
Galactic gatherings bring friends near.
Sip by sip, the universe sings,
In the laughter and love that each brew brings.

Infinite Inspiration in a Cup

In a mug where ideas brew,
Laughter swirls like the morning dew.
Stirring dreams with a sugar spoon,
I sip the stars beneath the moon.

Jokes percolate, they dance and play,
Baristas crack wise, hipster ballet.
Espresso thoughts zoom in the air,
Latte art that's beyond compare.

Sipping wisdom from a festive cup,
Spilling laughter, never give up.
Join the chatter, take a seat,
In this café, life feels so sweet.

Cheers to the brew and the cosmic cheer,
Every sip brings the universe near.
With each gulp, let the madness rise,
As we caffeinate the starlit skies.

Beanpot of the Universe

A pot that brews the galaxy's blend,
Frothy dreams with a side of trend.
Beans from Mars, milk from the Moon,
Stirring up fun, come taste the tune.

Spoonful of laughter, spice of the night,
Coffee so rich, it's purely outta sight.
Aliens drop in for a taste test,
With cosmic lattes, they'll feel blessed.

Each cup tells stories of travels afar,
Espresso shots under a twinkling star.
You might find Jupiter's roast quite bold,
But Earth's got that homey warmth, behold!

Grab a seat at this swirling affair,
Sip the universe, without a care.
In this beanpot, we find delight,
With every sip, the world feels just right.

Galactic Flavor

In a mug where galaxies collide,
Flavor explosions, take a ride.
Stardust sprinkles, a funky taste,
Interstellar sips, no need to waste.

Planets align in a frothy dream,
Cosmic cocoa, a quirky theme.
Black hole biscuits, and comet scones,
Nibbling on laughter, we're never alone.

Sip by sip, the universe beams,
In every gulp, a million dreams.
Rocket fuel with a splash of fun,
At this café, it's never done.

So raise your cup, toast to the skies,
With every drink, our spirits rise.
In galactic flavors, we extend our fate,
Together we laugh, and celebrate!

Eclipse of the Bean

In the shadow of a steaming cup,
Beans collide, liftoff ready, yup!
While the world takes a caffeinated pause,
Here's to sipping without a cause.

Moons of cream swirl in playful arcs,
Sunshine sweetness, igniting sparks.
Sip the eclipse, let the brew unfold,
This bean dance is a sight to behold.

With cosmic puns flying overhead,
Jupiter's roast gets our laughter fed.
Pour another round, don't spill a drop,
In this playful orbit, we just can't stop.

So gather round, as flavors confide,
In the eclipse of the bean, we'll glide.
Here's to fun, where joy meets the mug,
In this coffee show, we all snug!

The Milky Way Café

In a café far from here, drinks pour with cheer,
Star-shaped cookies dance, the galaxies near.
Planets serve a latte, black holes brew tea,
Sip a cosmic blend, taste infinity!

Comets slide on dishes, a tasty delight,
Martian muffins rise, they take off in flight.
Asteroids are crumbs, that tumble and roll,
Eating in space? Now that's rock and roll!

Time's a funny thing, it brews slow and fast,
A sip here lasts eons, how long 'til it's passed?
Lunar lights flicker, as laughter erupts,
We raise our mugs high, in this galaxy of cups!

So come take a seat, where the stars all abide,
The Milky Way Café is an interstellar ride.
With humor on the menu and coffee divine,
Join us in orbit, where we all intertwine!

Interstellar Java

At the edge of the void, there's a brewing surprise,
Where astronauts giggle and float in the skies.
Rocket-fuel coffee, a jolt to the core,
Even space squirrels stop in for more!

Starry-eyed patrons sip mocha and dreams,
Doughnuts on meteorites, wild as it seems.
Caffeine-powered ships sail through time and the night,
Every sip sends you soaring, oh what a flight!

Sip a cup of stardust, it's frothy and bright,
Baking under moonbeams gives pastries new height.
Galactic trade secrets, in a mug or a cup,
Naps in zero gravity? You can't get enough!

So cheers to this place, where the universe brews,
With beans from Andromeda, it's all from the views.
As planets collide, we all share a laugh,
In this interstellar joint — our favorite path!

Nebula Nights

Under swirling colors, the starlight shines fast,
Nebula nights filled with coffee and laughs.
Mars made us espresso, while Jupiter's sweet,
With Saturn's ring donuts, it's quite the treat!

Laughter fills the air, like sparks in the void,
Aliens dance, all the chaos enjoyed.
Wormholes in the corner, brewing something strange,
Space-time bends and twists, oh what a change!

Comets toast with cups, in a chaotic swirl,
Celestial cheerleaders do a dance and twirl.
Intergalactic humor, jokes light as a plume,
In our nebula café, we banish the gloom!

So when night falls down, and the stars shine bright,
Join the jovial crowd, in this cosmic delight.
With froth and a giggle, we banter and sip,
Nebula nights give the universe a flip!

Lattes Under the Aurora

Beneath the green curtains of aurora so bright,
Latte art dazzles, a whimsical sight.
Cosmic sprinkles dusted on pastries galore,
Even the sunbeams are begging for more!

Astro-bakers serve slices, galactic in shape,
With every sweet bite, a story to scrape.
Celestial cappuccinos? Yes, please, oh my!
We whisper to comets, as they giggle by.

With each frothy sip, the universe winks,
As quarks tease the cups, the cosmos just blinks.
Floating among laughter and stardust divine,
This whimsical haven is truly sublime!

So after you've danced with the stars overhead,
Join us for lattes, bring joy to your head.
Under the aurora, where fun never flocks,
We toast with our mugs — the cosmos unlocks!

Starlit Brews

Under a sky of twinkling lights,
Brewed a potion of curious sights.
Each sip a star, bursting in flight,
Gather 'round, it's a taste of delight.

Aliens dance in the coffee steam,
Whispering secrets, it feels like a dream.
With every gulp, we giggle and beam,
Oh, what a wild, interstellar theme!

Planets swirl in a frothy delight,
While comets zoom by, getting a fright.
We laugh as we sip, oh what a sight,
In our mugs, the universe feels just right.

So grab your cup and join this spree,
Where laughter erupts like a caffeinated glee.
From distant worlds, come sip with me,
In this joyous land of caffeinated jubilee.

Celestial Sips

Frothy clouds in mugs so round,
While rocket ships buzz all around.
Giggles erupt amidst the sound,
Every sip makes the cosmos astound.

Starry-eyed baristas with playful wit,
Mixing up drinks that seem to emit.
Laughter bubbles, oh what a hit,
A sprinkle of joy in every bit.

Space whales glide on cosmic foam,
As we sip and make this place our home.
With each tasty sip, we freely roam,
In this bubbly galaxy, we brightly comb.

So raise your mug to the night so wide,
Where aliens join us, side by side.
With delight in our hearts, we'll not hide,
In our whimsical world, let's coincide.

Lunar Latte Dreams

Latte art shaped like a moonlit face,
Playing tricks in this delightful space.
With every sip, we find our place,
In the laughter of interstellar grace.

Gravity may wane, but spirits are high,
As meteors race across the sky.
Chattering cups, oh my, oh my!
In stardust flavor, we boldly fly.

Whimsical beans from a galaxy far,
With hints of laughter, we twinkle like stars.
Each cup is magic, it's truth and bizarre,
Join us in rapture, no need for a car!

So steep in the joy, let the flavors bloom,
Defying gravity, we dance in the room.
With every refill, there's more to consume,
In this dreamland of lunar perfume.

Moonlight Mugs

The moon grins wide, sipping a brew,
As starry friends gather, a lively crew.
With laughter filling every venue,
In our moonlight mugs, happily askew.

Jupiter stirs with a giggle so bright,
Mixing up drinks in the soft, silver light.
We toast to the comets, in flight or in sight,
As we sip together, all feels just right.

Even the asteroids join in with cheer,
Making our mugs overflow with good beer.
We giggle and chortle, as we persevere,
In this gathering where worries disappear.

So fill your cup high, let the night unfurl,
With moonlight hugs and a merry whirl.
Join the laughter, give it a twirl,
In our constellation, let friendship swirl.

The Serene Space of Sips

In a corner of the night, they brew,
Planets dance while sipping too.
Asteroids bounce in a jolly ride,
With mugs held high, they laugh and glide.

Venus spills and Mars makes a mess,
Jupiter jokes, it's quite the fest.
Galaxies swirl in creamy delight,
Cosmic laughter beams so bright.

Comets whiz past like baristas grand,
Espresso shots from the starry hand.
Lambda lying low, they sip and share,
Galactic grins in a stellar affair.

Time drips slow like espresso so bold,
Tales of the universe, glee to unfold.
With every sip, the cosmos sings,
In this lounge of wonders, joy takes wings.

Celestial Steeping

Teas brewed from stardust, delightfully neat,
Planets steeping, oh so sweet.
Sip slow like time in a twinkling jar,
While the sun winks, a glowing star.

Milky Way flavors, galactic blend,
Every sip brings a new trend.
Moons in froth, bubbling with glee,
A latte made of gravity, oh whee!

Laughing black holes, swirling with cheer,
Contemplating life, the end is near!
Sipping cycles, the whims of fate,
In the funny universe, we contemplate.

Pouring laughter into each telling cup,
With space cookies, we never give up.
Cosmic flavor, a celestial treat,
At this brewing bar, life's bittersweet.

Starlit Brews

Underneath the dazzling skies,
Coffee brews spark twinkling eyes.
Sidereal sips from cups aglow,
Every gulp fuels the cosmic flow.

Starry laughter dances above,
This milky brew is truly love.
Late night chats with Saturn's rings,
Finding joy in absurd things.

Floating dreams in steaming cups,
Galactic giggles over hiccuped ups.
Moon marshmallows bob in the heat,
Cosmic concoctions make life sweet.

With comet cream and asteroid jam,
Countless flavors, oh, what a slam!
Here every sip is a space ballet,
In starlit brews, we dance away.

Celestial Conversations

Gathered around a cosmic table,
With planets spinning, we're all able.
Jovial tales and humor so grand,
As galaxies swirl, we understand.

A moonbeam joke, slick and light,
Cracking up through the endless night.
Witty quips from the stars above,
In this gathering, there's endless love.

Nebulae nod with a knowing wink,
Sipping knowledge while we think.
Interstellar banter flows like streams,
In the universe, we chase our dreams.

Chatter of beings from distant lands,
Trading funny, whimsical strands.
With every mug shared, we grow quite wise,
In celestial corners, laughter flies.

Celestial Café Chronicles

In a galaxy far, oh so bright,
Aliens sip lattes, what a sight!
Barista with three eyes, quite the flair,
Spills a mocha, we all stop and stare.

A comet zips past with a twist of lemon,
Sipping stardust, now that's a gem!
Martians play chess, their pawns made of cheese,
As Saturn's rings dance like a breeze.

Jupiter's latte, colossal and bold,
Milky Way muffins, stories untold.
Planets debating, who brews it best?
Coffee that's light-years ahead of the rest.

In this quirky place where starlight gleams,
Galactic giggles spark wild dreams.
With each cup served, laughter takes flight,
Join the fun in this cosmic delight!

Brewed Horizons

Beans from Orion, ground with a smile,
Sip by the stars, let's stay for a while.
Asteroids float by, holding a brew,
They wink at the barista, "Make one for two!"

A nebula stirs in a frothy delight,
While comets are dancing, all through the night.
Saturn rings donuts, sprinkled with glee,
Every bite's a blast, taste the decree!

Black holes for espresso, deep and so strong,
With a side of quasar, you can't go wrong.
Bubbles of laughter in every good cheer,
As light-years collapse, we have nothing to fear.

So take a sip from the universe vast,
Time stops for coffee, let's make it last.
With friends from afar, sharing tales that astound,
In this brewed haven where joy knows no bound!

Nebulous Nosh

Grains from the stars, baked with a grin,
We dine on delights where the fun begins.
Hungry for laughter, we feast on puns,
While sipping on bubbles, all things are fun!

Frappés from Venus, sweet as a dream,
Galactic pancakes, stacked to the brim.
With syrup from Saturn, we pour it on thick,
Not a single frown, just a cosmic kick!

Silly smoothies from Pluto take flight,
As Martians sing karaoke, a quirky sight.
Starfruit splatters, giggles around,
In this hangout where joy is profound.

Join the fiesta, with flavors galore,
As laughter erupts, we all want more!
In our space diner, the stars shine bright,
Nebulous nosh keeps our spirits light!

Astral Accents

With cups of starlight, we toast the night,
Every sip glimmers, a shimmering sight.
Raspberry comets swirl in our bowls,
While space-time bends and giggles extol.

Lunar tarts filled with wishes and dreams,
Each bite is a burst of wild, cosmic beams.
Friends from afar, we play interstellar,
Winning at charades, oh what a feller!

Nebula nachos, cheesy and grand,
We munch 'til we burst, without a bland strand.
Jupiter's juice flows like a stream,
With every guffaw, we float in a dream.

So gather your crew on this swirling ride,
Where laughter erupts and joy cannot hide.
In this vibrant realm where fun reigns supreme,
Ride the waves of laughter, chase every gleam!

Espresso Across the Universe

A comet brews in cups of light,
While planets spin in pure delight.
Supernova in a latte swirl,
Galaxies froth and freely twirl.

Milkshake moons do dance and play,
With starry straws that whisk away.
A rocket shot, it jolts the night,
Unleashing laughter, a playful fright.

Aliens sip from mugs so vast,
Debating whose beans brewed the best blast.
Cosmic baristas craft each dream,
While meteors crash, and planets scream.

With every drop, a giggle flows,
As light-years drift and laughter grows.
From nebulae to distant suns,
Espresso ignites and fills with fun.

Galactic Gatherings

In a café made of starry beans,
Martians mingle with moonlit queens.
Jupiter's jolt meets Saturn's curl,
With every sip, the cosmos twirl.

Conversations dip and dive like stars,
A wormhole opens—where are we, Mars?
Bright-eyed beings, on their space trip,
Trade stories over a frothy sip.

Asteroids bobbing with coffee cups,
Ursa Major mixes espresso ups.
Comets crack jokes with fiery tails,
As laughter sails on solar gales.

Black holes slurp with a gurgled cheer,
While distant worlds lend an ear.
Galaxy friends in a caffeinated daze,
Gathering stardust and silly ways.

Mocha Mysteries

In the depths of a nebula's brew,
Mocha whispers secrets, just for you.
A sprinkle of stardust, a hint of thrill,
Unraveling wonders with each warm chill.

Wormhole brews with a wry delight,
Mixing flavors under the starlit night.
Aliens ponder, what's in this blend?
A puzzle, a riddle, but never the end.

Strawberry comets join in the fun,
While black holes joke about races run.
With every taste, a new tale spins,
As laughter swells, the mystery grins.

Cosmic quirks in a cup so round,
Bubbles rise and laughter's found.
Sipping tales from places afar,
Mocha mysteries in the quirkiest bazaar.

Stardust Sips

A galaxy swirls in a cup so sleek,
With stardust sprinkles, laughter's peak.
Saturn's rings twist like whipped cream,
In this silly space, nothing's as it seems.

Coffee beans from a comet's tail,
Each sip a journey, a cosmic trail.
Jovial elves brew cups with flair,
As laughter bubbles in buoyant air.

With every taste, the universe beams,
Galactic giggles fuel wild dreams.
Each sip a trip on a comet's ride,
As joy and mischief, together, collide.

Starlight glimmers in espresso shots,
Frothy giggles and cosmic knots.
In this bizarre café, all coalesce,
Sipping stardust, embracing the jest.

Galaxies in a Teacup

Stars swirl in my mug, oh so hot,
Planets dance while I sip the lot.
A comet's tail whips past my nose,
I laugh at the galaxy that overflows.

Milky Way foam, a cappuccino crest,
Sipping stardust, I feel so blessed.
Jupiter's cream, Saturn's sweet spice,
Each sip brings laughter, oh so nice!

Nebulas down to caramel swirl,
With every gulp, my imagination unfurl.
I raise my cup to a distant star,
"Drink up, my friends, let's go far!"

In this little café, gravity bends,
Where laughter and caffeine are the best of friends.
Galaxies bubble, and we feel alive,
In the teacup universe where giggles thrive.

Astral Aromas

Brewed nebula, oh what a delight,
With every whiff, I'm taken to flight.
Asteroids crunch as I munch a cookie,
In this café, life's a bit funky!

Java beans from a distant moon,
Sipping space lattes that make me swoon.
I spill a bit on my cosmic shirt,
And laugh as gravity tries to flirt.

Bubbling black holes in my coffee cup,
With each swirl, I can't help but sup.
Kicking back on my fluffy star seat,
The universe winks—this drink is sweet!

When I finish my cosmic brew,
I promise to share it, oh yes, it's true.
Come join the fun, spread joy like foam,
In this starlit café, we've found our home!

Nebulae and Nectar

A splash of nectar from comet's tail,
Dancing flavors that will never pale.
Swirling bright colors in every cup,
What's that? A shooting star just gave a sup!

The rich aroma of cosmic delight,
Clouds of sugar that are light as night.
I giggle with stars, we've got secrets to share,
Spilling stories, floating high in the air.

Planet marshmallows bobbing about,
My coffee is wild, there's never a doubt.
Sip a bit slowly, let the flavors expand,
In our stellar café, we boldly stand!

As laughter rings through the galactic haze,
We'll toast to our follies in whimsical ways.
With each silly sip, joys come unbound,
In this universe sweetened, happiness found!

Universe Underfoot

My feet rest lightly on a starry floor,
With each step, I hear the cosmos roar.
Sip a little nectar, feel the vibe,
As galaxies giggle, they come alive!

Dust bunnies of stardust scatter wide,
Tripping on comets, I glide with pride.
The universe winks; it's all in the game,
A chaotically fun, caffeinated fame!

Within this café, I'm never alone,
Friends from the cosmos, we've all grown.
Every joyful laugh resonates above,
Floating with friends in a storm of love.

With each little sip, I feel so spry,
A universe beneath me, I soar and fly.
So grab your cup, let's laugh and play,
In this great adventure, we find our way!

www.ingramcontent.com/pod-product-compliance
Lightning Source LLC
Chambersburg PA
CBHW051659160426
43209CB00004B/950